The Ultimate
Sloth
Book for Kids

100+ Amazing Sloth
Facts, Photos & More

Jenny Kellett

Copyright © 2023 by Jenny Kellett

The Ultimate Sloth Book for Kids
www.bellanovabooks.com

ISBN: 978-619-92219-8-3
Imprint: Bellanova Books

All rights reserved. No part of this book may be reproduced in any form by any electronic or mechanical means including photocopying, recording, or information storage and retrieval without permission in writing from the author.

CONTENTS

Introduction 4
Sloth facts 6
Three-toed sloths 10
    Brown-throated sloth 12
    Maned sloth 14
    Pale-throated sloth 16
    Pygmy sloth 18
Two-toed sloths 20
    Linnaeus's two-toed sloth 22
    Hoffmann's two-toed sloth 24
More sloth facts 26
Sloth Quiz 68
    Answers 73
Word search 74
    Solution 76
Sources 77

INTRODUCTION

They're famously lazy and undeniably cute, but how much do you really know about sloths? Did you know they carry an entire ecosystem around with them? What about the 6-metre tall extinct giant sloth?!

We're going to learn more about these facts and many more. And don't forget to test yourself in our sloth quiz at the end.

Are you ready? *Let's go!*

SLOTH FACTS

Sloths are part of a group of mammals called *arboreal Neotropical xenarthran* mammals. **Arboreal** means that they live in trees, while **Neotropical** is a biogeographic region that makes up most of Central and South America. **Xenarthran** is a group of animals only found in the Americas. Other xenarthrans include armadillos and anteaters.

• • •

Sloths are famous for being really slow. They spend most of their lives just lounging around in trees.

Three-toed sloth.

A sloth hanging in a tree.

Sloths travel at a speed of around 0.24 km/h (0.15 mph) — making them the slowest animals on Earth.

There are two families of sloths: *Bradypus* (three-toed sloths) and *Choloepus* (two-toed sloths).

• • •

Although scientists originally thought all sloths were in the same family, they realized there were so many differences between two- and three-toed sloths that they split them into two families.

So let's take a look at the differences between the two types.

THREE-TOED SLOTHS

Scientific name: *Bradypus*

There are four subspecies of three-toed sloths: the brown-throated sloth, the maned sloth, the pale-throated sloth, and the pygmy three-toed sloth.

The easiest way to tell three-toed and two-toed sloths apart is by the number of digits on their hands and feet. Three-toed sloths have three fingers and toes on each hand and foot.

Three-toed sloths also have short tails, while two-toed sloths' tails are even shorter and can barely be seen.

They are diurnal, meaning they are most active during the day and sleep at night.

BROWN-THROATED SLOTH

Scientific name: *Bradypus variegatus*

The brown-throated sloth is the most common species of three-toed sloths.

They usually have paler faces than other sloths, with very dark patches under their eyes.

They have greyish-brown to beige colored hair, with a darker patch on their throats.

Range of the brown-throated sloth. Image: *IUCN Red List.*

MANED SLOTH

Scientific name: *Bradypus torquatus*

The maned sloth can only be found in southeastern Brazil.

They have small heads and a long outer layer of hair, which is usually pale brown to gray in color.

They get their name from the long black mane of hair that runs down their neck and shoulders.

Range of the maned sloth. *Image: IUCN Red List.*

Credit: Paulo B. Chaves

PALE-THROATED SLOTH

Scientific name: *Bradypus tridactylus*

The pale-throated sloth is very similar to the brown-throated sloth, except its throat is a lighter color, and they are much rarer than the brown-throated sloth.

You will usually find pale-throated sloths in the tropical rainforests of north-eastern South America.

Range of the pale-throated sloth. *Image: IUCN Red List.*

PYGMY SLOTH

Scientific name: *Bradypus pygmaeus*

The pygmy three-toed sloth is also known as the monk sloth or dwarf sloth. It is an endangered species, which can only be found in the mangroves of Isla Escudo de Veraguas, an island off of Panama. They were only recognized as a species in 2001.

Range of the pygmy sloth.
Image: IUCN Red List.

As its name suggests, the most noticeable feature of the pygmy sloth is its small size — they are smaller than other sloths.

Image: Fundación Almanaque Azul

They look very much like the brown-throated sloth in color and features, but are around 40% smaller.

They mostly eat leaves from the red mangrove trees found on their island.

TWO-TOED SLOTHS
Scientific name: *Choloepus*

There are two subspecies of two-toed sloths: Linnaeus's two-toed sloth (*Choloepus didactylus*) and Hoffmann's two-toed sloth (*Choloepus hoffmanni*).

Despite the name, two-toed sloths actually have three toes on their back legs, and two on the front.

Two-toed sloths look quite different from three-toed sloths. They have much shorter tails, but larger ears, heads and hind feet than three-toed sloths. Their hair is also longer and their eyes much larger than three-toed sloths.

LINNAEUS'S TWO-TOED SLOTH

Scientific name: *Choloepus didactylus*

Linnaeus's two-toed sloth is also known as the southern two-toed sloth or unau.

They are found in several countries in northern South America, including Venezuela, the Guyanas, Colombia, Ecuador and Peru.

Linnaeus's two-toed sloth has a dark throat, but is otherwise very similar to Hoffmann's two-toed sloth.

Range of the southern two-toed sloth
Image: IUCN Red List.

THE ULTIMATE SLOTH BOOK

HOFFMANN'S TWO-TOED SLOTH

Scientific name: *Choloepus hoffmanni*

Hoffmann's two-toed sloth is found in a much smaller area than the southern two-toed sloth. They enjoy the mature rainforests around northwest South America and southern Central America.

Range of Hoffmann's two-toed sloth
Image: IUCN Red List.

Image: Geoff Gallice

They were named after the German naturalist who was one of the first to identify them.

Hoffmann's two-toed sloth has a pale neck, which makes them easy to identify.

There are five subspecies of Hoffmann's two-toed sloths, each of which can be found in a different region.

MORE SLOTH FACTS

As well as the many types of sloths that we have just looked at, other species also used to exist, including the ground sloth. The ground sloth, as the name suggests, lived on the ground and was common in Cuba and other parts of the Caribbean, until around 11,000 years ago.

• • •

The tallest of the giant ground sloths (known as **Megatherium**) stood at over 6 meters (19.7 ft) tall!

A depiction of the elephant-sized giant ground sloth (*Megatherium*).

Both two-toed and three-toed sloths can be found in the same forests. Usually, there will be one species of each living in a particular area.

Nobody actually knows exactly how long sloths live, because they are so hard to track in the wild. However, the oldest known sloth in captivity was almost 50 years old.

∙ ∙ ∙

Sloths regularly fall out of trees! However, like cats, they are built to survive the falls. In fact, they can fall over 100 ft (30.48m) without being harmed.

∙ ∙ ∙

When male sloths are fighting over a female, they will often try to knock each other out of a tree to win her.

A wild three-toed sloth.

A sloth's coat consists of a short layer of soft underfur and a top layer of thicker, longer, shaggier hairs.

∙ ∙ ∙

Sloths have cracks in their hairs that allow algae to grow inside them and turn them a greenish color, which helps them to camouflage themselves!

∙ ∙ ∙

Two-toed sloths are nocturnal, while three-toed sloths are diurnal.

∙ ∙ ∙

Sloths will often lick their hair to get extra nutrients from the algae. However, sloths never groom themselves—which helps the algae grow better.

The algae growing in a sloth's coat have been found to contain bacteria that may help in the cure for cancer.

• • •

As well as algae, sloth moths also live in the sloth's coat. Some species of these moths live entirely off the nutrients within the sloth's fur. And there's more!

There's an entire ecosystem growing within a sloth's coat. From beetles and mosquitoes to ticks and mites — there can be dozens of species of arthropods living on a sloth at any one time. They feed off of the algae.

Sloths aren't able to control their body temperature like many animals. This helps to preserve energy, but also means their body temperatures can change rapidly over the day. If the temperature gets too cold, the microbes in their stomachs can no longer help them to break down their food, and they can starve to death even on a full stomach.

...

The metabolic rate of a sloth is the slowest of any animal in the world. It can take around 30 days for a sloth to digest a single leaf!

A sloth's stomach is about 30% of its body weight. It has four chambers and is almost permanently full.

• • •

Being slow works out well for sloths. They only need to eat a low-energy diet of leaves, and it protects them from predators, such as cats, who are on the lookout for fast-moving animals. Sloths can only move about two meters per minute on the ground.

• • •

Although sloths are almost helpless on the ground, they can swim if they need to.

Three-toed sloth hanging around on a branch.

THE ULTIMATE SLOTH BOOK

Can you see the algae growing on this three-toed sloth? Image: Jack Charles

Sloths can swim three times faster than they can move on the ground. They usually do the backstroke.

• • •

Sloths are on average 60-80 cm (24 to 31 in) long, with two-toed sloths usually being slightly larger than three-toed sloths.

• • •

They're hard to see, but sloths do have ears. They are tiny and usually covered in hair, which is why they have such bad hearing.

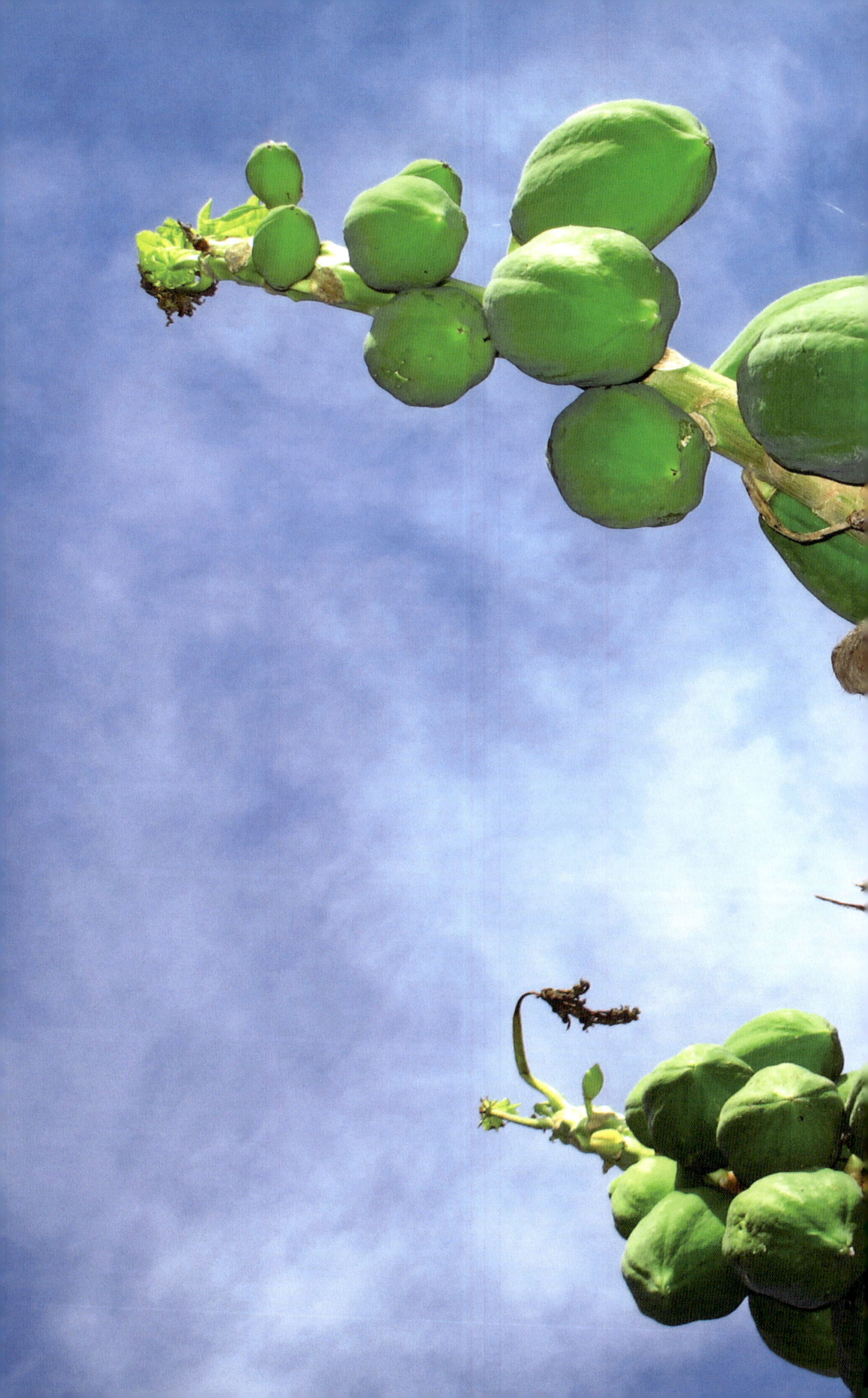

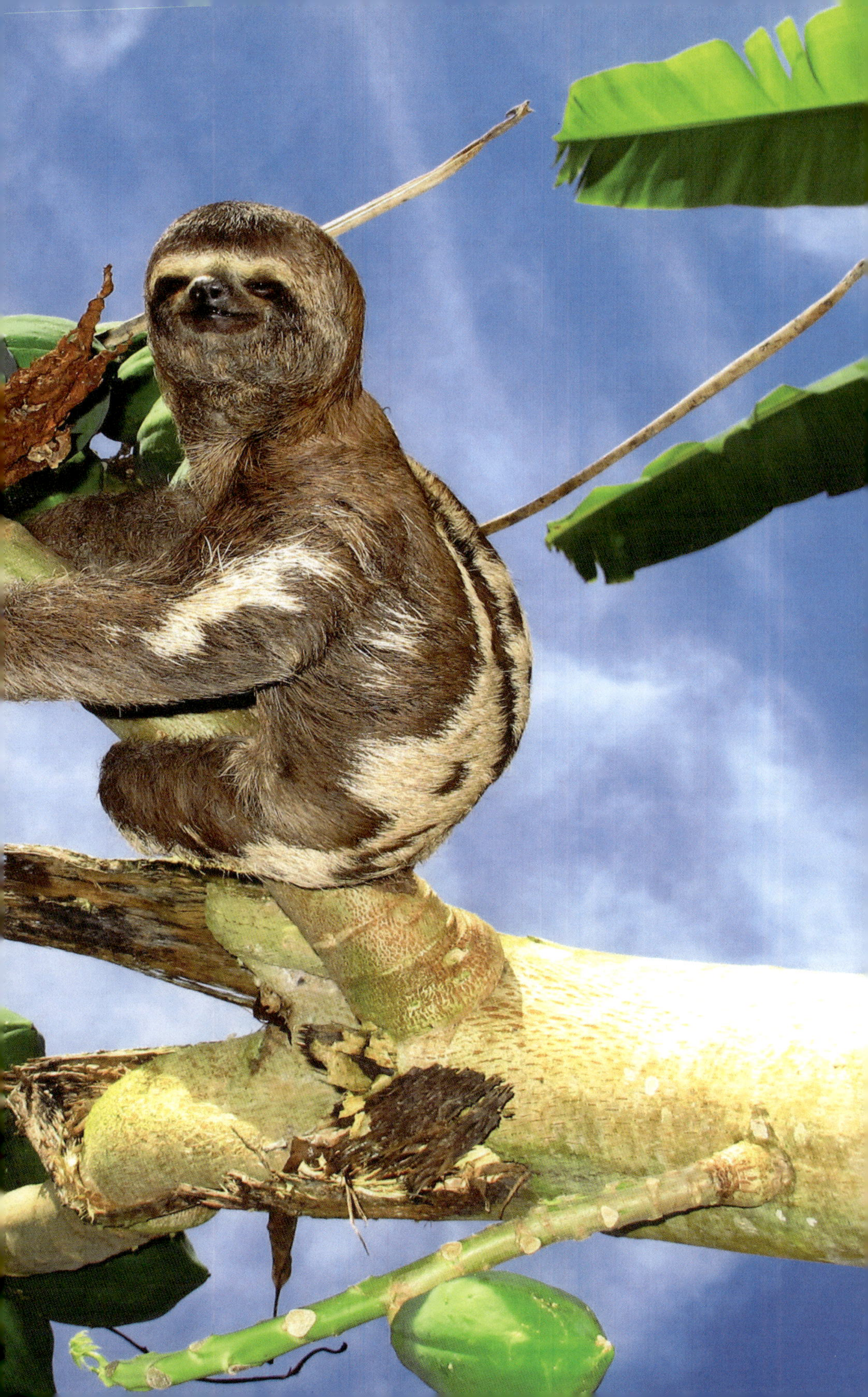

Sloths are almost blind. They rely on smell and touch for finding their way around and searching for food.

· · ·

Sloths can't fart.

· · ·

Sloth babies are called... sloth babies!

· · ·

Almost all mammals have seven cervical vertebrae (the spine bones in the neck). However, sloths have between 5-7 (two-toed sloths) and 8-9 (three-toed sloths). The only other mammal not to have seven is the manatee, with six.

Close-up of a two-toed sloth baby.

The extra vertebrae at the bottom of a sloth's neck help it to turn its head on a 270° axis, giving them almost 360° vision without needing to move its body.

· · ·

A sloth's hair grows in the opposite direction to other mammals. In most mammals, the hair grows outwards towards their extremities (hands, feet, head). But, because sloths spend so much time upside down their hair grows away from them!

· · ·

Although sloths spend most of their time hanging from trees, their limbs aren't designed to support much weight. Instead, they are made for hanging and grasping.

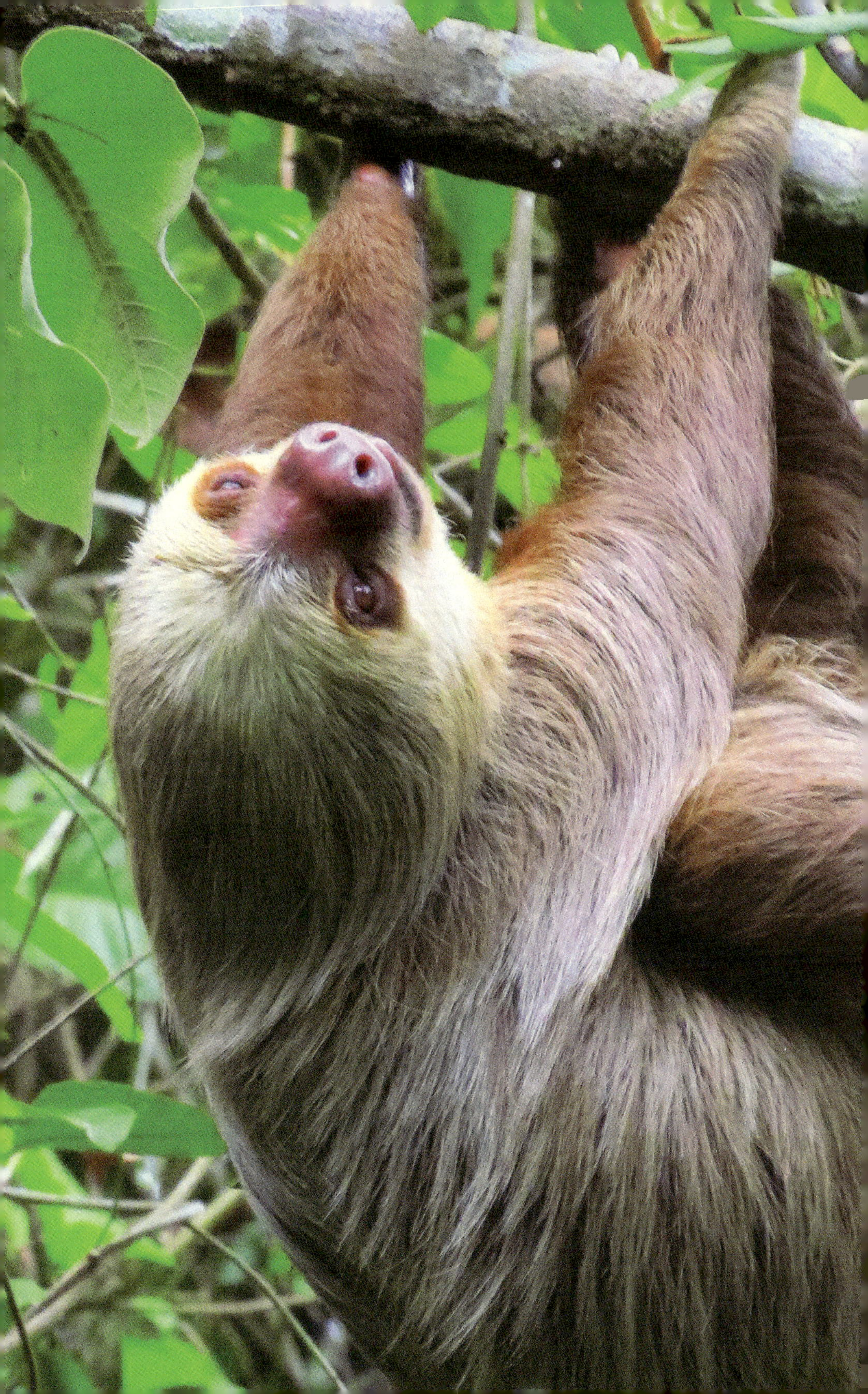

THE ULTIMATE SLOTH BOOK

Image: Sebastien Molinares

Their famously long claws keep them secure on branches with very little effort. They are held on so tight, that even after death they remain hanging there.

• • •

While most mammals' muscle weight is around 40-45% of their body weight, for a sloth it is only 25-30%.

• • •

The arms on a three-toed sloth are around 50% longer than their legs. They are more evenly matched on two-toed sloths.

It is hard to tell the difference between male and female sloths. Many zoos have received the wrong gender of sloth because of this!

• • •

Sloths are able to hold their breath for around 40 minutes so that they have enough time underwater to cross rivers or go to different islands.

• • •

Sloths are solitary creatures and spend most of their time completely alone, except during the mating season. Occasionally, females will meet up with one another.

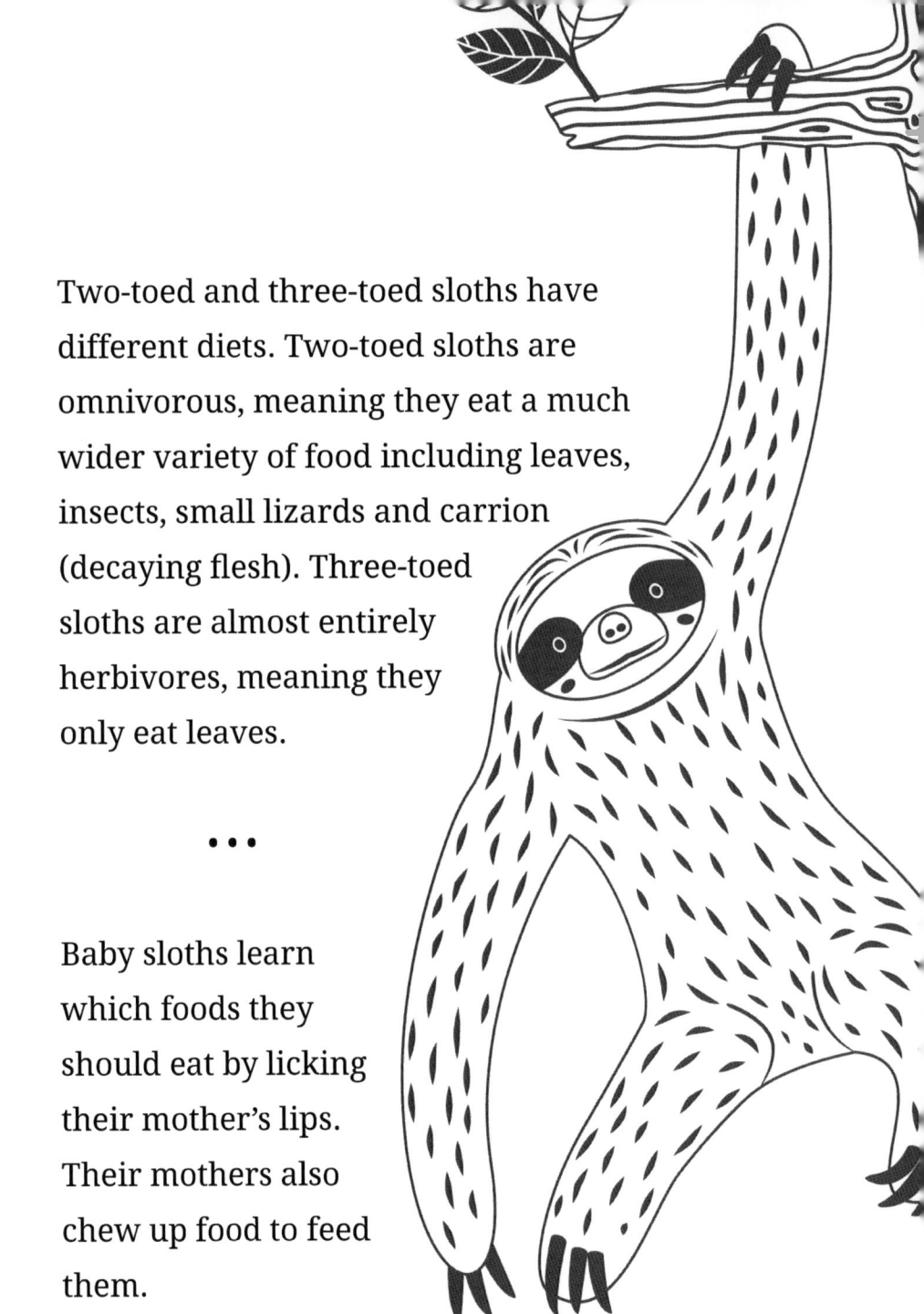

Two-toed and three-toed sloths have different diets. Two-toed sloths are omnivorous, meaning they eat a much wider variety of food including leaves, insects, small lizards and carrion (decaying flesh). Three-toed sloths are almost entirely herbivores, meaning they only eat leaves.

...

Baby sloths learn which foods they should eat by licking their mother's lips. Their mothers also chew up food to feed them.

Unlike two-toed sloths, three-toed sloths go down to the ground when they need to go to the toilet. They usually go once a week and always in the same spot. Scientists are very confused by this behavior, as it makes them very vulnerable to predators.

• • •

The mating season also varies between the different sloths. Pale- and brown-throated sloths usually mate during a specific time of the year, while maned sloths will mate throughout the year.

Two-toed sloth.

THE ULTIMATE SLOTH BOOK

Claws of a two-toed sloth baby.

Sloths only give birth to one baby at a time.

・・・

Sloths give birth while hanging upside down!

・・・

After mating, the male sloth plays no part in the baby sloth's life. The mother takes care of them.

・・・

The gestation period (the time that a female is pregnant) is six months for the three-toed sloth and 12 months for the two-toed sloth.

Sloth babies stay with their mothers until they are around five months old, clinging onto their abdomens for safety.

• • •

Babies are able to cling to their mother's fur just moments after being born.

• • •

Baby sloths are born fully formed, covered in fur and with their eyes open, ready to get life started!

• • •

Female sloths usually have one baby per year, although their slowness can mean it takes them longer to find a mate!

Two-toed sloths are only 340 grams (12 ounces) when they are born. Three-toed sloths are just slightly larger.

• • •

Sloths can't be kept as pets, as their habitat is so specialized.

Sloths have very thick skin, which helps them to survive changes in temperature and dangerous falls.

• • •

Sloths only poop once a week, so when they do go they can lose almost a third of their body weight in one go!

• • •

Over half of all sloth deaths occur while they are going to the toilet. This is because they come down from the trees and are in danger of predators.

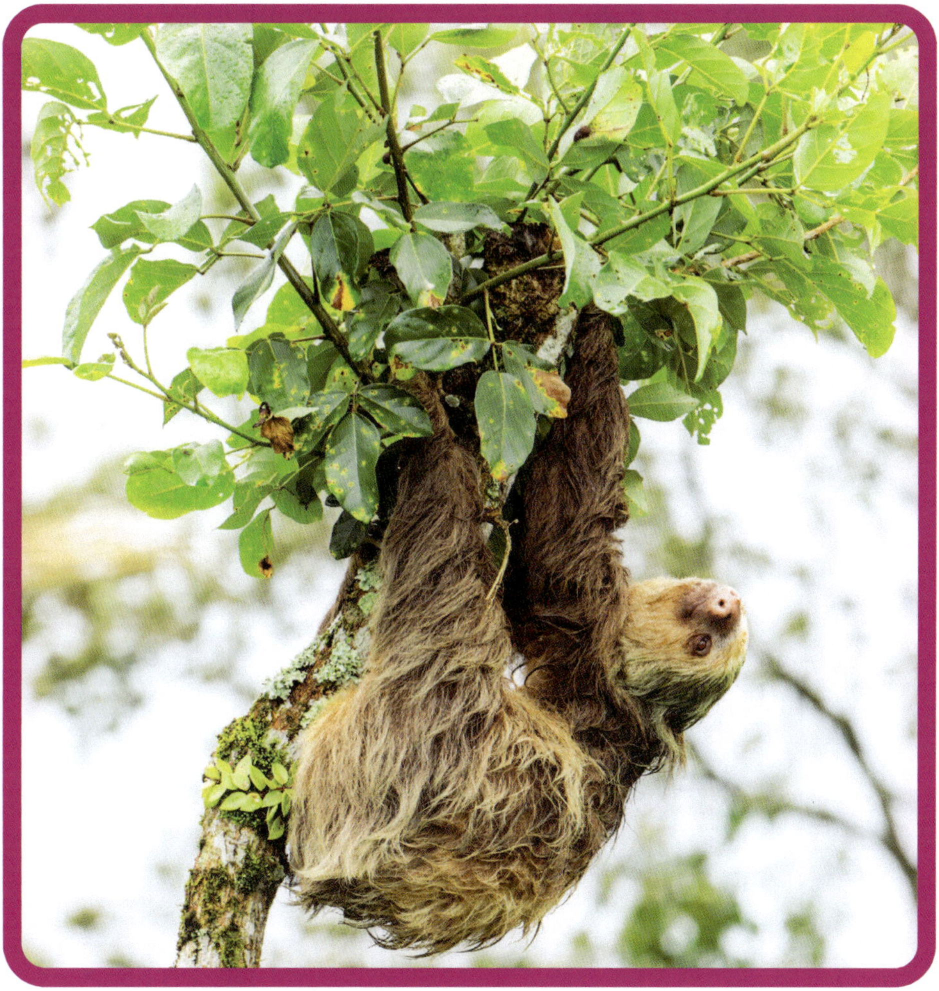

Before doing their business, sloths do a little dance, which scientists like to call the 'poop dance'.

• • •

Sloths are three times stronger than most humans. They can lift their entire body weight up with just one arm!

• • •

A sloth's internal organs are attached to their ribcage, which makes it easier to hang upside as the weight of the organs doesn't restrict their breathing.

Although sloths spend a lot of time not moving, they aren't always sleeping. In the wild, they sleep around 8-9 hours a day. However, in captivity, they sleep much longer — around 15-20 hours.

• • •

Sloths permanently look like they're smiling! However, don't mistake this for happiness. Even if they are in pain they still look like they're smiling.

• • •

There have been cases where sloths have accidentally mistaken their arms for branches, and then fallen off their tree. Oops!

THE ULTIMATE SLOTH BOOK

A female three-toed sloth carrying her baby.

Sloths don't sweat, nor do they have a particular scent. This keeps them safe from predators.

• • •

Although sloths are usually very quiet, females let out a loud scream when they are ready to mate. It sounds like a loud 'eeeeeeh'.

• • •

Three-toed sloths can't be kept in captivity, as they are picky eaters and can only survive in their natural habitat.

Sloths have long tongues that they can stick out 10-12 inches (25-30cm).

• • •

Sloths rarely drink water, as they get all the water they need from leaves. However, occasionally you might see a sloth drinking from a river or lake.

• • •

Each year on October 20th sloth-lovers celebrate *International Sloth Day*. So how do you celebrate this day? You can donate to an organization that helps the endangered pygmy sloth, raise awareness about the problems they face, or perhaps just laze around for the day!

Even after a baby sloth leaves its mother, it will continue to live in the same area and communicate with her through calls.

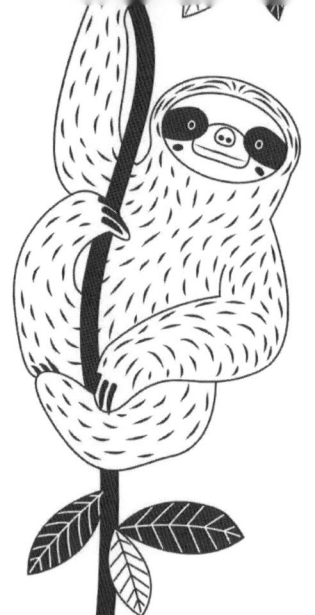

• • •

Sloths have very interesting teeth. Their teeth grow continuously throughout their lives and have no enamel on them. Also, unlike most mammals, their teeth are much smoother and rounded in shape.

• • •

Although not all sloths are endangered, most are at risk of habitat loss. As rainforests are chopped down, sloths lose places to live.

Three-toed sloths generally sleep in the forks of trees, while two-toed sloths prefer to hang from the branches.

• • •

Sloths are generally safe from predators while they are in their trees, but it's a different story when they're on the ground. Predators include jaguars, anacondas, other big cats, ocelots and eagles.

• • •

If a sloth meets a predator on the ground, it can not run away. It relies on its sharp claws and teeth to try and stay safe.

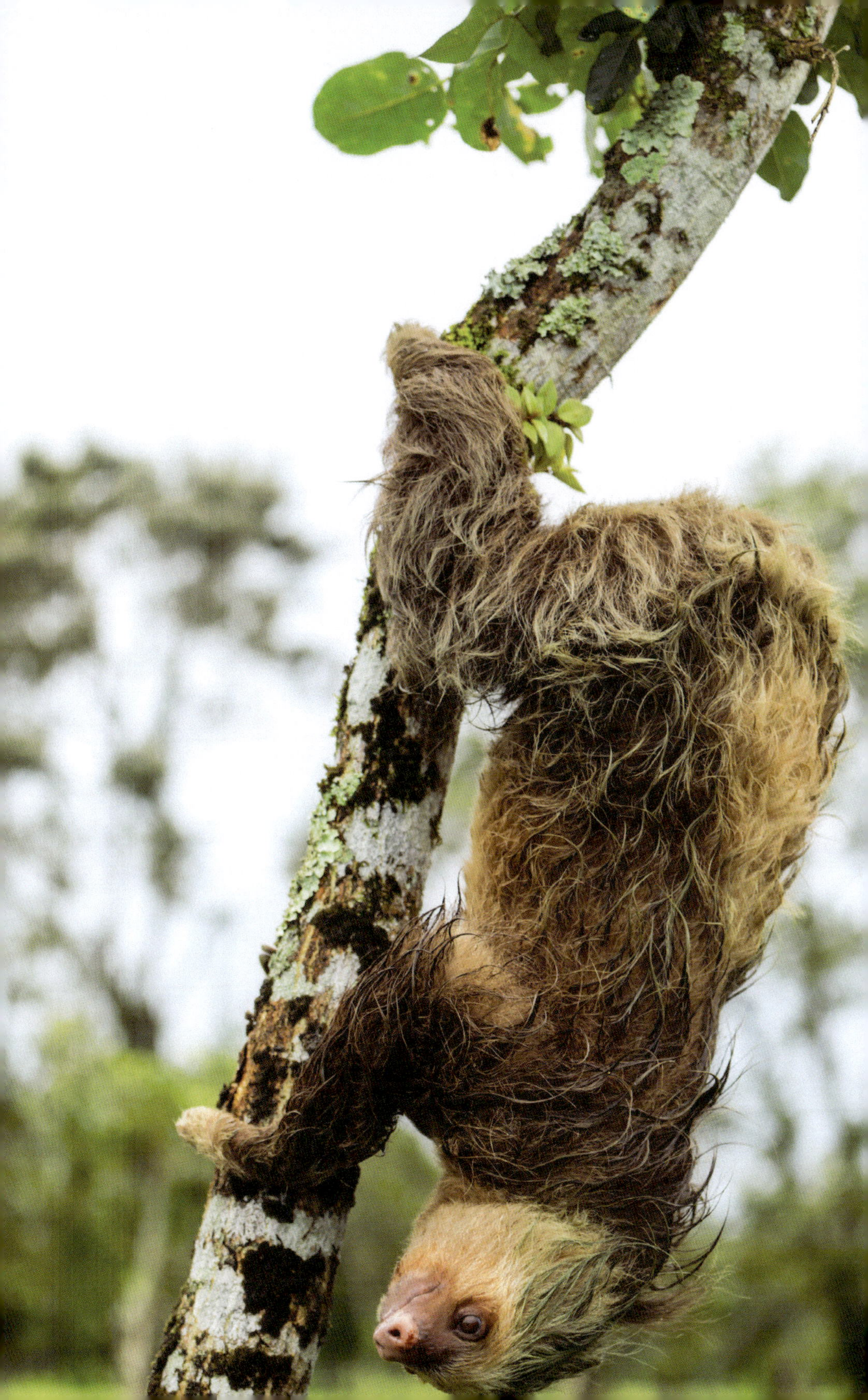

There is no reported case of a sloth ever killing a human. Even minor injuries are very rare.

• • •

There are many places where sloths are used as props for tourist selfies. This is very stressful for them and can shorten their lifespan dramatically. It is important that if you want to see sloths in the wild that you don't pick them up or disturb them.

• • •

The sloth's closest relative is the anteater. They both have long claws, but while sloths are mostly herbivores, anteaters are insectivores (they eat only insects).

Some sloths spend their entire lives living in the same tree.

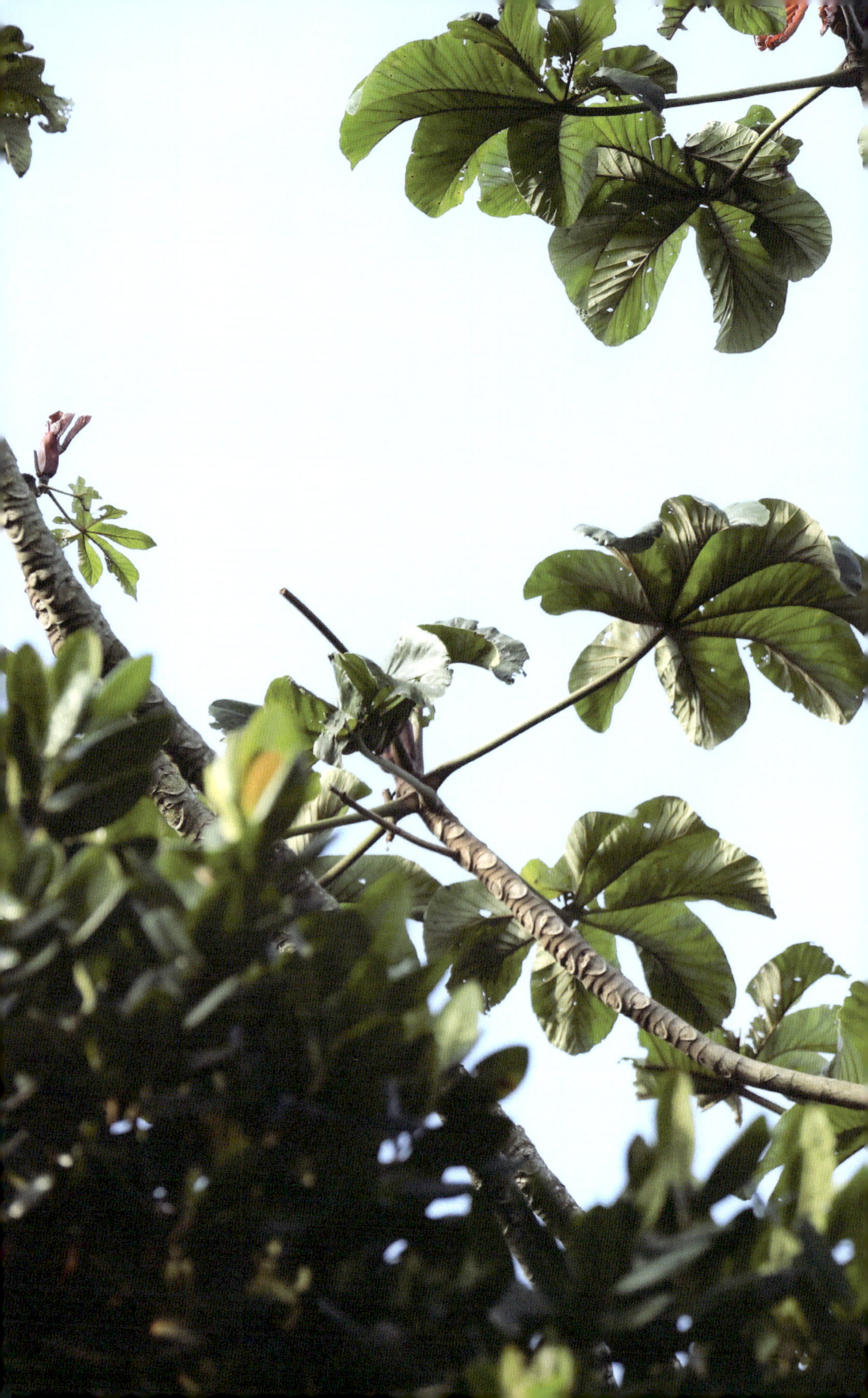

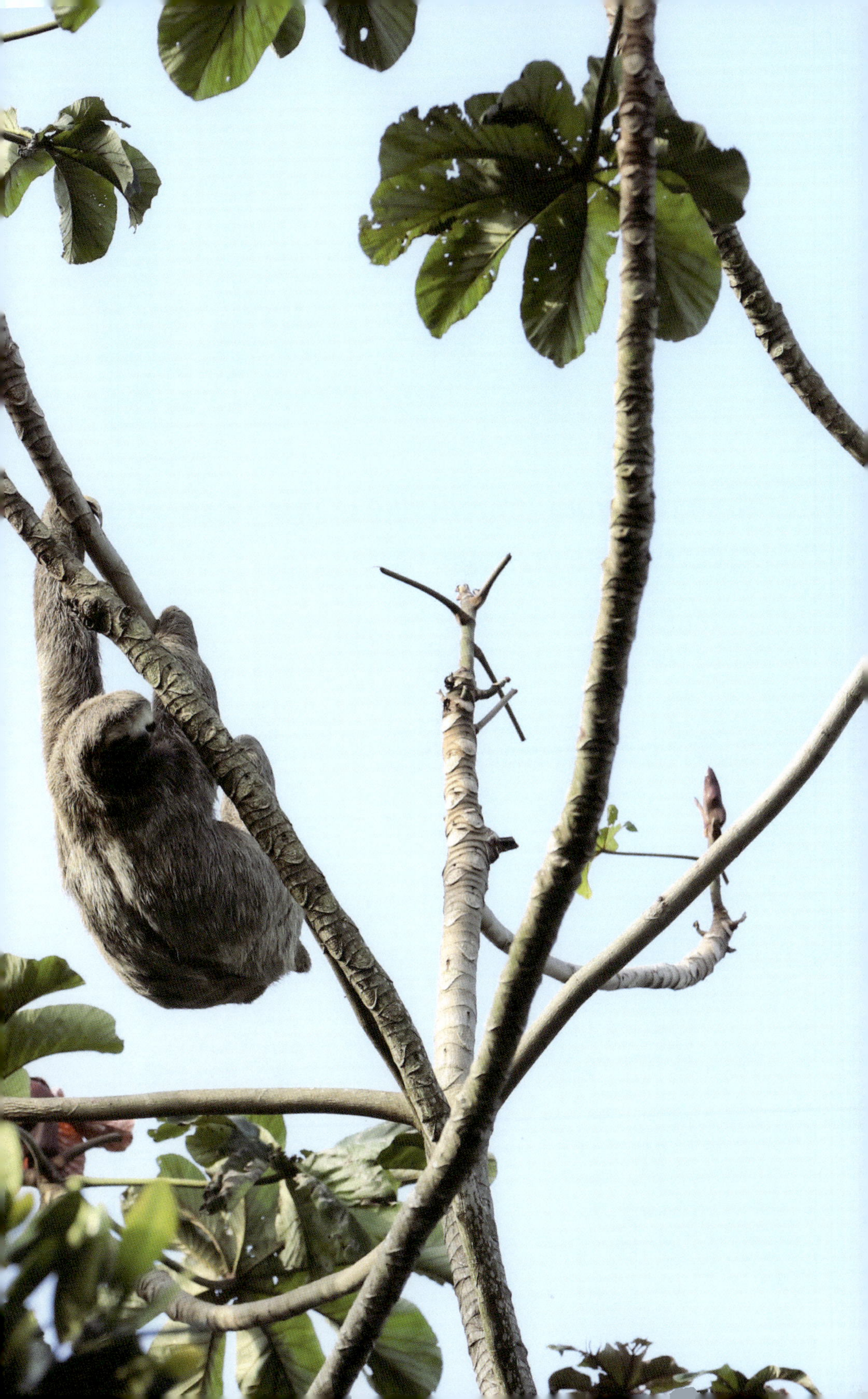

THE SLOTH QUIZ

Now test your knowledge in our Sloth Quiz! Answers are on page 73.

1. What are baby sloths called?

2. Which is usually bigger — two-toed or three-toed sloths?

3. Sloths can swim faster than they can walk. True or false?

4. How do male sloths try to impress females?

5. Where can pygmy sloths be found?

6. How many toes do two-toed sloths have?

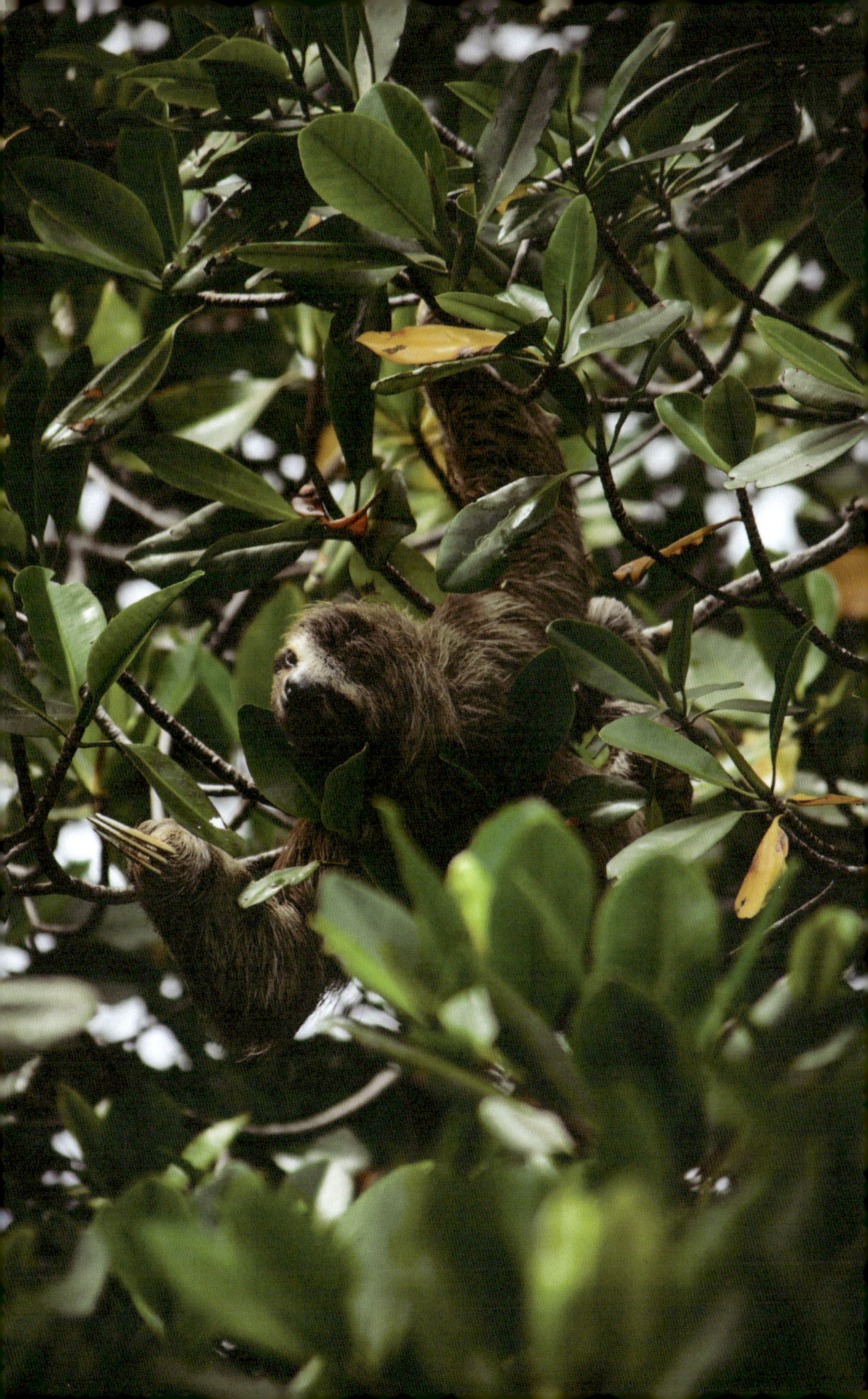

7 Where does the maned sloth get its name from?

8 Which is the most common species of three-toed sloth?

9 Can you name the two types of two-toed sloth?

10 What is the scientific name of the extinct giant ground sloth?

11 What do three-toed sloths eat?

12 How long does it take for a sloth to digest a single leaf?

13 What senses do sloths use to search for food?

14 For how long can sloths hold their breath underwater?

15 What day is International Sloth Day?

16 How many babies do sloths have at a time?

17 How long are female two-toed sloths pregnant for before they give birth?

18 When a sloth poops, how much of its body weight does it lose?

19 How much stronger are sloths than most humans?

20 What animal is the sloth's closest living relative?

A female brown-throated three-toed sloth. Image: Sharp Photography

ANSWERS

1. A baby sloth!

2. Two-toed sloths.

3. True.

4. By knocking other males out of trees.

5. Isla Escudo de Veraguas, an island off of Panama.

6. Three.

7. The long black mane that runs down its neck.

8. The brown-throated sloth.

9. Hoffmann's and Linnaeus's two-toed sloths.

10. Megatherium.

11. They are herbivores, so they eat leaves and other plants.

12. 30 days.

13. Smell and touch.

14. Around 40 minutes.

15. October 20th.

16. One.

17. 12 months.

18. One-third!

19. Three times.

20. Anteater.

Sloth WORD SEARCH

```
W Y T E Z C B T J U P D
F C Y T E S J H D S V T
S L O T H A T E D F I H
S A Y H F D L H T G U R
A W G E S P Y G M Y T E
J S B M N R Z D A E E E
H G R A I N F O R E S T
D E F W B C R Q A U F O
E A L A Z Y G F D P E E
S N M A D F G E Z D S D
Z M A M M A L F W A D G
X Q J H F D S R J N B C
```

Can you find all the words below in the wordsearch puzzle on the left?

SLOTH CLAWS MAMMAL

BABY THREE TOED LAZY

RAINFOREST ALGAE PYGMY

THE ULTIMATE SLOTH BOOK

SOLUTION

		C								T
S	L	O	T	H	A					H
		A				L				R
		W			P	Y	G	M	Y	E
		S	B				A			E
			R	A	I	N	F	O	R	E	S	T
				B						O
			L	A	Z	Y				E
										D
		M	A	M	M	A	L			

SOURCES

"BBC Radio 4 - Radio 4 In Four - 10 Incredible Facts About The Sloth". 2021. Bbc.Co.Uk. https://www.bbc.co.uk/programmes/articles/34C4dGp1kqnbs5MT7TZQN44/10-incredible-facts-about-the-sloth.

"Sloth - Wikipedia". 2021. En.Wikipedia.Org. https://en.wikipedia.org/wiki/Sloth.

"Linnaeus's Two-Toed Sloth - Wikipedia". 2021. En.Wikipedia.Org. https://en.wikipedia.org/wiki/Linnaeus%27s_two-toed_sloth.

"Ground Sloth - Wikipedia". 2021. En.Wikipedia.Org. https://en.wikipedia.org/wiki/Ground_sloth#Extinction_in_North_America.

"Sloth | Definition, Habitat, Diet, Pictures, & Facts". 2021. Encyclopedia Britannica. https://www.britannica.com/animal/sloth.

"10 Facts About Sloths, Nature's Slowest Animals". 2021. World Animal Protection. https://www.worldanimalprotection.us/news/10-facts-about-sloths-natures-slowest-animals.

HowStuffWorks, Animals, Animals, Mammals, Mammals, Do week?, Do poop?, Do spot?, Do poop?, and Why slow?. 2018. "Sloths Only Poop Once A Week — But They Make It A Good One". Howstuffworks. https://animals.howstuffworks.com/mammals/sloths-only-poop-once-week.htm.

"13 Chill Facts About Sloths". 2018. Mentalfloss.Com. https://www.mentalfloss.com/article/559749/facts-about-sloths.

"Attempt To Export Nearly-Extinct Pygmy Sloths Sets Off International Incident In Panama". 2013. Mongabay Environmental News. https://news.mongabay.com/2013/09/attempt-to-export-nearly-extinct-pygmy-sloths-sets-off-international-incident-in-panama/

"The Sloth Institute – Do Sloths Drink Water?". 2021. Theslothinstitutecostarica.Org. http://www.theslothinstitutecostarica.org/sloths-drink-water/#:~:text=It%20is%20true%20that%20sloths,licking%20water%20off%20of%20leaves.&text=So%20as%20this%20video%20shows,a%20rare%20sight%20to%20see!.

"**Fun Sloth Facts For Kids - Interesting Information About Sloths**". 2021. Sciencekids.Co.Nz. https://www.sciencekids.co.nz/sciencefacts/animals/sloth.html.

"**Why Are Sloths Slow? And Six Other Sloth Facts**". 2021. World Wildlife Fund. https://www.worldwildlife.org/stories/why-are-sloths-slow-and-six-other-sloth-facts.

Naish, Darren. 2012. "The Anatomy Of Sloths". Scientific American Blog Network. https://blogs.scientificamerican.com/tetrapod-zoology/the-anatomy-of-sloths/.

"**10 Facts About Sloths**". **2021.** World Animal Protection. https://www.worldanimalprotection.org.uk/blogs/10-facts-about-sloths.

"**Baby Sloth - Animal Facts Encyclopedia**". 2021. Animal Facts Encyclopedia. https://www.animalfactsencyclopedia.com/Baby-sloth.html.

"**Pygmy Three-Toed Sloth | EDGE Of Existence**". 2015. EDGE Of Existence. http://www.edgeofexistence.org/species/pygmy-three-toed-sloth/.

We hope you learned some awesome facts about sloths!

We'd love to hear from you in a *review*.

Not only do they make us smile, but they help other readers find the right books to buy. Thank you!

You can also visit us at
www.bellanovabooks.com
for more great books.

ALSO BY JENNY KELLETT

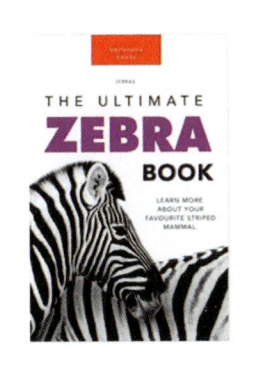

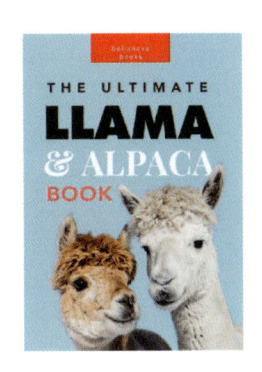

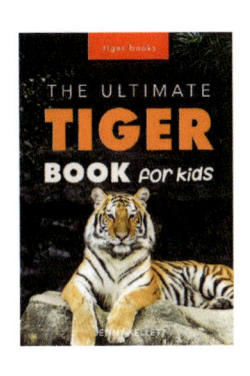

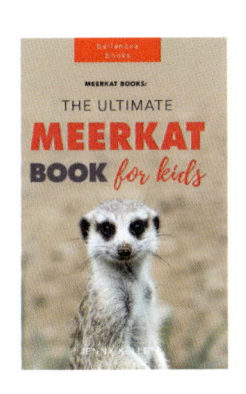

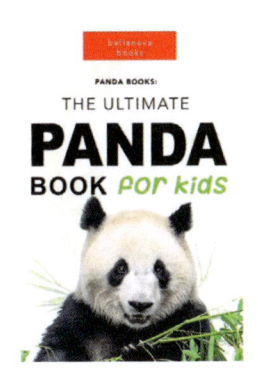

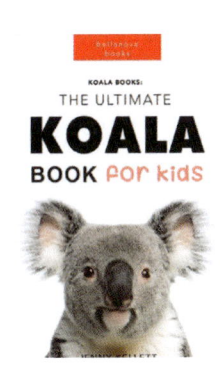

... and more!

AVAILABLE IN ALL MAJOR ONLINE BOOKSTORES AND AT WWW.BELLANOVABOOKS.COM

THE ULTIMATE SLOTH BOOK

Printed in Great Britain
by Amazon